How Does God Express His Sovereignty?

Larry Adams

Copyright © 2019 Larry Adams, All Rights Reserved

Scripture quotations marked NASB are taken from the New American Standard Bible®, Copyright © 1960, 1962, 1963, 1968, 1971, 1972, 1973, 1975, 1977, 1995 by The Lockman Foundation Used by permission." (www.Lockman.org)

Dictionary Quotations marked (CWSB Dictionary) taken from The Complete Word Study Bible Dictionary. Copyright © 2003 by AMG Publishers. All rights reserved.

ISBN: 978-0-9893460-0-9

Contents

Basic Concepts	1
What Are We Missing?	7
Embellishment And Exaggeration	10
God's Curse On Modifying His Word	12
Believe versus Repent	14
How Can We Know God's Ways?	16
What Are God's Ways?	18
The Beatitudes	19
Other References To God's Ways	22
God Is A Warrior	26
Control Can Be Satanic	28
Sovereignty Twists	31
Context Is Everything, And Then Some...	37
In Summary...	45

Other Books by Larry Adams

Six Biblical Issues Against "God Is In Control"
Discipling A New Believer
Revelation: A Fresh Perspective
Did You Ever Realize...
Future Focus
That Your Prayers May Not Be Hindered
Out On A Limb

How Does God Express His Sovereignty?

Basic Concepts

In my book, "*Six Biblical Issues Against "God Is In Control"*, " I addressed the issues of both God can control some things and has chosen not to control people, and under those conditions how can things take place. The one thing that was not investigated was if God's sovereignty is not dependent on absolute control of every breath and quiver of everything, then how does God express, or implement, His Sovereignty? Does the Scripture give us any indication of what God has to say about Himself and how He does things, and what are the characteristics of what He does and how He does things that would be Scripturally recognizable as being or belonging to God? The focus of this book will be a discovery of what is in Scripture that reveals answers to these questions.

Most Christians believe that "God is Sovereign" in at least the sense that He is the Creator and ultimate King and authority of the entirety of the universe, at least for all that we can see and determine that exists. There are some that take this to an extreme that God is constantly, unrelentingly, causing everything to happen, and without that "control" of absolutely everything, nothing would exist, much less have any activity. Of course, there's also the extreme other end of the spectrum that believes God has nothing to do with anything, much less does He exist. We're only going to examine the situation of God being involved in His creation, the other extreme will have to wait for another time and place.

Among those who believe in some degree of God's Sovereignty, there are many variations, almost too many to consider without a supercomputer. Since I only have access to a laptop, we'll have to select only a few of those

How Does God Express His Sovereignty?

degrees for consideration. There is one extreme degree that believes God's Sovereignty is based on such total control that God is the only possible cause and means by which anything can happen, such as, our breathing, and an insects flapping wings as it targets your neck. I've dealt with that idea in my book "*Six Biblical Issues Against "God Is In Control,*" " and this will not be taken into account in this discussion. For those who wander around in the middle of the Sovereignty/Control spectrum, there is a confusing situation that seems to have everyone baffled; God is completely Sovereign, and mankind is totally responsible for their actions and choices, i.e. their sins. In all the writings I've read on this particular issue, there is something missing in their presentation and argument. The basis of the conflict and confusion about how can He be in total control and we are totally responsible for our sin is because of their concept of control.

Those writers are very emphatic about the co-existence of these two elements at the same time and at the same place or situation. The missing element in their arguments and presentations is a question that should be obvious but is the kind of thing that gets lost very quickly in the emotional intensity of the issue. That question is simply, "How does God express or implement his sovereignty?" Please be careful here and not mix in "How people think God should express His sovereignty." What we think is irrelevant, we do not dictate to God what He does and does not do. Only what God does and says has any bearing on anything of God. The Scripture references presented in those writings are very compelling in their "proof" of the existence of God's Sovereignty along with mankind's responsibility. I get the same impression from most of the writers that they have their own "world view" or "world context"

How Does God Express His Sovereignty?

from which they are writing, but it is impossible to determine just what is their full picture of God's Sovereignty. I have known people who are multi-millionaires who live in a modest house, not in a gated community, drive moderately priced cars, and from all outward expressions are simply middle class, not wealthy. I know others who seem to live on a budget of at least $10,000 a week – a completely different form of expression of wealth. This is part of the question we should be asking – how does God express or implement His Sovereignty?

There are some "christianeze" terms that are not found in Scripture but are useful and convenient in discussing theological issues. Some of these are "Trinity" and "Rapture." Augustine came up with the terminology of "Doctrine of the Trinity," way back in the late AD300's, early AD400's. The word "trinity" is never used in Scripture but is very convenient in discussions. The word "Rapture" is a derivative of "caught up" from the Latin Vulgate translation of Scripture; there are no words used in the Greek New Testament that can be directly translated by the English word "rapture." My strong suspicion is that the term "Sovereignty" falls into this same category. In the Old Testament, there is an English word used in translation that is either sovereign or sovereignty. The word in Hebrew simply means "kingdom," and by inference, "ruler." There is one use of sovereign in the New Testament that simply means "ruler." These two meanings don't come anywhere close to the current theological meanings of Sovereignty. The modern theological meanings of Sovereignty are based on the concept of "God is in control," and have varying degrees of how much control really exists, depending on which denominational dialect is currently in use.

The only objection to the use of the word "Sov-

How Does God Express His Sovereignty?

ereignty" that I have is that there are too many varying shades of meaning associated with it, and no one seems to care to define what they really mean by the term. With some of the writers, it seems like there are multiple possible ways of defining what they mean by the term, and that confusion and uncertainty as to what it really means, does not seem to disturb them. In many cases, the same writer in the same article uses the term "sovereignty" in ways that are contradictory to each other, and that writer doesn't seem to recognize the contradiction. Is God a God of chaos? We can define "Trinity" and "Rapture" with very minor variations, but "Sovereignty" does not have a reasonably consistent definition among all the groups that use it. Let me be clear about my own meaning of the term "Sovereignty." That is simply that God is the best, greatest, most powerful ruler and creator and authority of the universe and anything else within or without that universe. That meaning would be acceptable by most "Sovereignty" enthusiasts as a part of what it should mean – they would usually add much more, significantly more than the basic meaning in the Hebrew of "kingdom." From what I have read and studied in depth in the Scriptures, my perception of the difference between my meaning and theirs is simply the matter of how God chooses to "express" or "implement" his position of authority and power. This will be the focus of this discussion.

    There is one other issue that needs to be identified before we get into the "heart" of the matter. The most well-known label for this issue is "reading something into the text." In classical logic, this falls under the titles of "argument from absence," or "argument from ignorance," or "argument from silence." These terms may be used interchangeably in the following discussion. These four terms

How Does God Express His Sovereignty?

basically mean that the text has no information in either direct words or proper inference within the context that describes a concept that people want the text to state.

An example is in Genesis chapter 2 where God says that it is not good for Adam to be alone, a helper compatible with him is needed. God then makes the animals and Adam names them, but none are suitable for Adam. Then God causes sleep to come on Adam, and God extracts a rib and fashions woman from it. Some will use this situation to come to the conclusion that "God is in control" because God did not ask Adam's permission to put him to sleep and take a rib - God just did it to Adam because "God is in control." The problem is that the text does not provide any information one way or the other about "asking permission." This is an argument from absence and is fallacious illogic. True evidence is never "absent." Evidence is always something that exists, and if one would want to "prove" something does not exist, there would need to be an overwhelming amount of examples where the item is actually absent before being able to state that the item is really not there. Sometimes it might be the case where just one item has not been found yet.

An example of this would be determining if a coin is "double-headed" by flipping it a thousand times and it always comes up heads and never tails. It would be easier to physically examine the coin, but if it is not possible to perform a physical examination, then the results of flipping it a thousand times and always coming up heads and never tails would be an acceptable substitute to define the coin is double-headed. Typically, the number of heads and tails on a regular coin would be near 50% each. Argument from absence is an attempt to use something non-existent as though it was for real. This is fallacious illogic and is used

How Does God Express His Sovereignty?

frequently to "substantiate" theological doctrines.

How Does God Express His Sovereignty?

What Are We Missing?

In analyzing the condition of Christianity in the US, I came up with my list of the top five things most Christians ignore. These are:

1) God's commands (His rules and regulations on relationships);

2) God's will (His wish, desire, intent, with no concept of demand; the things which are pleasing to Him, the things which make Him happy);

3) God's ways (the how and why He does the things He does based on who He is);

4) God's voice (He speaks to us for many reasons, one of them being how to apply the principles and concepts within His word);

5) God's word (His principles and concepts by which He wants us to live and which represent His character and personality).

For over 1,000 years (since Augustine in the late AD300's to early AD 400's) theologians have mixed God's commands with God's will as though they had never looked up the meaning of the word that the Holy Spirit inspired in the Greek New Testament. God's commands and God's will are two totally different concepts. God's commands could be likened to a General giving orders to his troops, while God's will could be likened to someone deciding which flavor of ice cream to have for dessert. Perhaps that may be a bit simplistic, but you should get the point.

God's ways are frequently dismissed because of a misunderstanding of one word in Greek in the phrases, "unsearchable judgments," and "unfathomable ways," in Romans 11:33. The word in Greek for "unsearchable" and

How Does God Express His Sovereignty?

"unfathomable" means "cannot be figured out," it does not mean "cannot be known." There should be an obvious difference between "figured out" and "known." Psalm 103:7 tells us that God made known His ways to Moses, and Luke 12:21 tells us that someone in the crowd told Jesus, "You teach God's ways." As God teaches us His ways, we can know His ways. But since His ways are higher (more excellent) than our fleshly, worldly ways, the ingenuity of our own minds is inadequate to figure them out.

Deuteronomy 30:15-16a (NASB) *"15 "See, I have set before you today life and prosperity, and death and adversity; 16 in that I command you today to love the Lord your God, to walk in His ways and to keep His commandments and His statutes and His judgments..."*

We cannot walk in His ways if we don't have a clue about them. God does not change – if He wants His people to walk in His ways back at Mt. Sinai, and Jesus taught God's ways, then He still wants us to know and walk in His ways.

God's voice is consistent within both Testaments. Deuteronomy 28 identifies two things about God's voice: "If you listen to the voice of the Lord your God," and many blessings follow. Then in 28:15, "if you do not listen to the voice of the Lord your God," and many curses follow. There are more than three times as many words devoted to the curses as to the blessings.

John 10:27 records Jesus saying, "*My sheep hear my voice...*" Listening to God's voice is important in both Testaments. God's voice is not the neurotic "booming voice in the head," like movies and science like to joke about. God's voice is something way down deep in our spirit, that all too often is easily ignored. God does not change, and His voice is just as important today as it was back at Mt.

Sinai.

How Does God Express His Sovereignty?

God's word, the Bible or the Scriptures, is our ultimate authority on God. His word contains the principles and concepts that we are to live by and represent God's character and personality. There are also many examples of both living rightly and wrongly, along with prophecy, that God has identified will happen in the future. We need His still small voice, the Holy Spirit living within us, guiding us and teaching us about how to apply the principles and concepts in specific situations in which we find ourselves. The Bible does not contain everything about every possible situation we might encounter, like what job should you have, or who is Mr./Ms. Right for you. How we apply God's principles and concepts depend on how much we know of His word and if we listen to His voice. There are too many Christians who never bring their Bible to worship services, and never read it during the week, and only pray "grace" at dinner at home. These ones never know His principles and concepts, never learn His ways, and certainty don't know that He has a voice.

God's ways are the key issue in understanding how God expresses or implements His Sovereignty. It's not just that God's Sovereignty exists (it really does), but how does He use it, how is it an expression of His personality and character, and authority and power? The answer to that question just might be very different from what most people's fleshly desires and the ingenuity of their minds would imagine.

How Does God Express His Sovereignty?

Embellishment And Exaggeration

Embellishment and exaggeration seem to be an integral part of how people understand words. The word "grace" is one of the most frequent words subject to embellishment and exaggeration. People add all kinds of characteristics and attributes to "grace" that really just don't exist. "Grace" simply means "kindness." The word "gift" also falls in this category of embellishment and exaggeration.

At the other extreme, people will suppress the existence of words in a sentence. The word "through" happens to be one of the words most frequently suppressed. In the following two passages these words are used and embellished and suppressed because of the carelessness with which we read. Carefully read these next two passages, noting the words that are underlined and the meaning of those words in brackets immediately following the underlined word. Then read them again, skipping the underlined word and read only the bracketed meaning in place of the underlined word. The second reading will give you a different impression of what Paul was really stating.

Romans 3:21-25 (NASB) "[21] *But now apart from the Law the righteousness of God has been manifested, being witnessed by the Law and the Prophets,* [22] *even the righteousness of God* through *[by means of] faith in Jesus Christ for all those who believe; for there is no distinction;* [23] *for all have sinned and fall short of the glory of God,* [24] *being justified as a* gift *[that which is given or granted] by His* grace *[kindness]* through *[by means of] the redemption which is in Christ Jesus;* [25] *whom God displayed publicly as a propitiation in His blood* through *[by means of] faith. This was to demonstrate His righteousness because in the forbearance of God He passed over the sins previously committed;"*

How Does God Express His Sovereignty?

Ephesians 2:8 (NASB) *⁸ For by grace [kindness] you have been saved through [by means of] faith; and that not of yourselves, it is the gift [that which is given or granted] of God;"*

When you read the meanings of the words in place of the words, you probably found a more practical understanding of what the Holy Spirit inspired through Paul. There are many reasons why we read carelessly, myself included. It can be tedious and somewhat difficult to pay attention to ALL the words we read and obtain the whole meaning of what is being read. We just don't want to spend the time doing it the right way, and we then get all kinds of different ideas about what God and salvation are all about. The following details of God's personality and character are usually ignored because of our careless reading that embellishes and suppresses things we read and frequently do both in the same sentence. Please take the time and read carefully, paying close attention to the context and the details.

Those two passages reveal to us that God is a loving and forgiving God who freely gives salvation to those who believe. (In case you were not aware, in the Greek, believe is a verb, faith is a noun, and both are derivatives of "persuade." The most basic definition of believe and faith is "to have a firm persuasion.")

How Does God Express His Sovereignty?

God's Curse On Modifying His Word

God has a curse on modifying His word. This is identified in Deuteronomy 4:2, 18:18-20; Proverbs 30:6; Jeremiah 26:2; and Revelation 22:18-19.

Deuteronomy 4:2 (NASB) "*² You shall not add to the word which I am commanding you, nor take away from it,...*"

Proverbs 30:6 (NASB)" *⁶ Do not add to His words Or He will reprove you, and you will be proved a liar.*"

Jeremiah 26:2 (NASB) "*² "Thus says the Lord, 'Stand in the court of the Lord's house, and speak to all the cities of Judah who have come to worship in the Lord's house all the words that I have commanded you to speak to them. Do not omit a word!!*"

Revelation 22:18-19 (NASB) "*¹⁸ I testify to everyone who hears the words of the prophecy of this book: if anyone adds to them, God will add to him the plagues which are written in this book; ¹⁹ and if anyone takes away from the words of the book of this prophecy, God will take away his part from the tree of life and from the holy city, which are written in this book.*"

The Deuteronomy 18 passage speaks the most clearly on this issue.

Deuteronomy 18:18-20 (NASB) "*¹⁸ I will raise up a prophet from among their countrymen like you, and I will put My words in his mouth, and he shall speak to them all that I command him. ¹⁹ It shall come about that whoever will not listen to My words which he shall speak in My name, I Myself will require it of him. ²⁰ But the prophet who speaks a word presumptuously in My name which I have not commanded him to speak, or which he speaks in the*

How Does God Express His Sovereignty?

name of other gods, that prophet shall die.' "

Verse 19 speaks to the one who listens to God's word through the prophet. Note that in several of the referenced passages that we are to pay attention to all of God's words, not leave out any, and not add to any of His words. Leaving out (omitting) or adding to what God has stated is effectively not listening to all His words. God will "require it of him," the one not listening. In Hebrew, the common understanding of this phrase was "make an inquisition of." I don't know about you, but personally, I would never want to be the focus of any kind of inquisition by God since He would be Judge, Prosecutor, and Executioner. I really don't think that would be a good thing... If we do not pay proper attention to all of God's word then we would obviously fall under this curse. Proverbs 26:2 tells us that "a curse without a cause will not alight." If we ignore or add to God's word, then there would be a valid cause... I'm sure you can figure out the rest...

How Does God Express His Sovereignty?

Believe versus Repent

Believing takes place in the heart, not the mind according to Scripture. I have an electronic Bible app that permits me to search for combinations of words, not only within a single verse but within a range of verses – you know the long run-on sentences that Paul uses that span as many as 10 or 12 verses??? This search capability permits me to find word associations within Paul's paragraphs, not just phrases. I searched for associations of "belie*" and "mind" within 10 verses and found no associations. (The wildcard format of "belie*" will find all forms of that – believe, belief, believed, anything beginning with "belie".) Doing a similar search on "belie*" and "heart" found these: Mk. 11:23, 16:14 Lk. 8:12, 24:5; John 14:1;Acts 8:37; Rom. 10:9-10. All this to say that the Bible does not munge or mix the concepts of heart and mind when it comes to believing, the Bible is not careless. 1 Corinthians 2:13, in the Greek, tells us that the Holy Spirit not only inspired or taught the words but how to express them (συγκρίνοντες.).

See these verses regarding repent: Heb. 6:1; Acts 2:38, 3:19, 5:31, 8:22, 11: 18, 17:30-31, 19:4, 20:21, 26:19-20; Mk. 1:4, 15; Lk. 3:3, 5:32, 13:3, 17:3, 4, 24:46-47; 2 Pet. 3:9. The Scriptures do not mix-up or confuse believe in the heart, and repent, a change of mind. Theologians will munge the two, but the Bible does not. Repent and believe do work together, but that does not mean they are one and the same thing, nor do they take place in both mind and heart in a confused manner.

The "popular" definition of repent, "turn from your sins and turn toward God," really does not fit either repent or believe, but "convert" in the Greek. This is something

How Does God Express His Sovereignty?

that is a work of the Holy Spirit which begins the instant of salvation. We take generalities and applications of a word's meaning and make unwarranted assumptions about things. This is very similar to the problem with embellishment and exaggeration. The confusion between repent and believe falls into the same category. This is just an example of not paying attention to all of God's word.

Our minds want to reduce and compress, summarize, the information we receive, And usually, this obscures important details. What we believe is first processed by the mind which provides an evaluation of the information. The heart will believe that evaluation. As you follow this discussion, you may have to "repent" about things you thought you already knew. Consider seriously what is actually written in Scripture is the truth, irrespective of any exaggerations or embellishments that are added on.

How Can We Know God's Ways?

God made known His ways to Moses, Jesus taught God's ways. Part of God's ways is represented by His commands, another part of His ways is represented by His will, and all of this is presented within his written word, the ultimate authority on who God is, His commands, and His ways. Deuteronomy 30:16 tells us that one of God's commands is to "walk in His ways." We must know them to walk in them. That is part of how we are to relate to God.

Psalms 95:9-10 (NASB) *"9 "When your fathers tested Me, They tried Me, though they had seen My work. 10 "For forty years I loathed that generation, And said they are a people who err in their heart, And they do not know My ways.""* (Also quoted in Hebrews 3:10.)

Here we see that God lays the blame for not knowing His ways on the error in the hearts of those who had to die in the wilderness – an error of the heart, an error in what they believed, was all it took. I cannot count how many people I have heard state that we cannot know God's ways. I cannot see the hearts of these people, only God can do that, but, I seriously wonder if their statements are really from the heart or just in their minds because of seriously erroneous teaching or deliberate deception. We may never know which it is. With the correct teaching, errors of the heart could be changed. People would then be able to be taught by God and know His ways.

Deuteronomy 32:4 tells us that His ways are just. Hosea 14:9 tells us that the righteous walk in His ways. Isaiah 55:8-9 tells us that His thoughts and ways are higher than our thoughts and ways – the reason why God needs to teach them to us and we cannot figure them out by the strength of our flesh and the ingenuity of our minds. Psalm

How Does God Express His Sovereignty?

25:4, 9 tells us that we can request God to show us His ways, and it is the humble whom He teaches His ways. Isaiah 2:3 tells us that He teaches us His ways so that we can walk in His paths. Isaiah 53:6 indicates that we all go astray by turning to our own way, it reminds me of Romans 3:23, all have sinned and have fallen short of God's glory.

That was six passages that indicate we really need to know God's ways, no doubt about it. And we need to be willing to let God teach us. If you are married, you know what it is like to learn the ways and habits and likes and dislikes of your spouse, and it takes time, perhaps several years. Learning the ways of God is also going to take time. Learning God's ways is more than just memorizing certain Scriptures or having a collection of facts and figures. God made mankind with emotions and will (desires, wishes, intentions) and God's ways are major insights to the same things in God Himself.

How Does God Express His Sovereignty?

What Are God's Ways?

The Ten Commandments are really a "two-sided coin." (Exodus 20) We usually look at them as rules of what NOT to do and the definition of sin (Romans 7:7). The other side of this "coin" is that God does not do those things either, and that is a huge insight into God's personality and character, the foundation of His ways. The opposite of murder is giving life. Coveting's opposite is rejoicing in the blessing of someone else. Each of the Ten Commandments has an opposite that reveals God's personality and character. God's ways give us a similar kind of insight to who is God.

In Luke 12:21, someone tells Jesus that He teaches God's ways. One of the teachings that help us in this respect is what is popularly called the "Beatitudes." We are to be holy because He is holy (1 Peter 1:16). If we are to follow the Beatitudes it is because God is that way also. God's ways are His personal insight to himself and the reasons why He does things the way He does. God does not tell us to be holy as He is holy and then himself behave in a different manner. That would disqualify God from being trusted, for anything, especially salvation.

How Does God Express His Sovereignty?

The Beatitudes

Matthew 5:3-12 is where we find the Beatitudes. The first one tells us that God does "not have an arrogant spiritual attitude," the meaning of "poor" – He is "poor in spirit."

Verse 4 tells us that those who mourn will be comforted. The word for "comfort" in the Greek is parakaleo which means "to call alongside for help." This is the basis of the idea Jesus discusses in John chapters 14 and 16 – the parakalatos, the Comforter, the Holy Spirit that would be given to the disciples after Jesus ascension – the one called alongside to help. God is a comforter and He is there at the side of each of His children. Psalm 121:1-2 tells us that our help comes from the Lord. God is our comforter, our guide, our teacher...

The next one in verse 5 tells us that God is humble and meek. Please be careful here and do not read into that what many think of those two words because of our particular modern culture – words can change meaning over time. In the first century and before, humble and meek were not indicators of weakness, but were words that indicated "ability under control," i.e. self-control, which is one aspect of the fruit of the Spirit in Galatians 5:22-23. Paul, in 2 Corinthians 10:1, identifies that Christ is meek and gentle. Jesus identified that He himself is humble in Matthew 11:29 and that if one sees him, that one has seen the Father in John 14:9, therefore God the Father is humble and meek.

Verse 6 shows us that God hungers and thirsts for righteousness or justice. This was formerly spelled "right-wiseness" which gets closer to the meaning of the word in the Greek – doing everything the "right way." There is a contrast presented in the New Testament regarding this word "righteousness." If you study the word "lawlessness" in the

How Does God Express His Sovereignty?

Bible, in the NASB it occurs 14 times, 2 in the Old Testament. Let's focus on the New Testament use of this word. Two times it is described as "lawlessness is sin," and "sin is lawlessness." These two really don't give us any practical meaning of the word, just a category for lawlessness. The other 10 uses of lawlessness tell us that it is "the intent of the heart to commit sin." This is the opposite of "righteousness," the intent of the heart to pursue holiness and justice, doing things God's way. God was displeased with that generation of Israelites because of the error in their heart which prevented them from knowing God's ways. Lawlessness prevents us from being able to know God's ways – we really need to be focused on righteousness just as God is.

The fifth one is "merciful," which means "actively compassionate." This involves not just outward activity that looks good, but those actions are driven by an internal attitude that desires those kinds of activity. While we were still sinners, God loved us and sent His son to die for us (Romans 5:8). God's love for us in His heart spurred Him into action. The active compassion we need in our hearts is to be the source of desire for righteous activity, just like God. Mercy and compassion are also identified in Exodus 33:19, quoted in Romans 9:15. Compassion is also identified in Deuteronomy 30:3, Judges 2:18, and 2 Kings 13:23. This is also the foundation in James chapter 2 for his statement that he will show (demonstrate) his faith by his works (the things he does).

The "pure" in heart will see God. "Pure" means without blemish, spotless, completely clean. God's heart is this way. We say that "imitation is the sincerest form of flattery." In God's scheme of things, imitation is the sincerest form of worship. Who and what does your heart worship? Is your heart a mix of righteousness and lawlessness? It needs to be only one way, pure, completely focused on God's ways based on an intimate relationship with God.

How Does God Express His Sovereignty?

The "peacemakers" will be called sons of God in verse 9. When God sent His son to die for the sins of the whole world, He was actively establishing the means of peace between people and God. We are to do likewise in both bringing God's peace in salvation to others and work at applying that peace between people. As Paul stated it, "*as far as it is possible with you, be at peace with all others* (Romans 12:18)."

The eighth one is in verses 10 to 12. In the eyes of the world, God is to blame for everything that "isn't right." This in spite of the fact that all that is "wrong" is because of sin that the world does not want to take responsibility for. God is persecuted by the world and sinners by taking His name in vain, blaming Him for whatever someone doesn't want to deal with. Many times when I have heard the phrase, "God is in control," the person is blaming God because a prayer wasn't answered, or a situation didn't turn out the way the person thought it should have. And the world and sinners will do the same for anyone who focuses their life on pleasing God. God endures the blame and rejection of the world, sinners, and the lies of Satan. We must do the same and be the ones who bring peace into the situation. This peace would obviously include the peace of the Gospel. If you are a believer in Jesus for salvation, then you have experienced the application of God's peace through the Gospel.

How Does God Express His Sovereignty?

Other References To God's Ways

The revelation of God's ways does not end with the Ten Commandments and the Beatitudes. Jeremiah 9:23-24 tells us:

Jeremiah 9:23-24 (NASB) "*²³ Thus says the Lord, "Let not a wise man boast of his wisdom, and let not the mighty man boast of his might, let not a rich man boast of his riches; ²⁴ but let him who boasts boast of this, that he understands and knows Me, that I am the Lord who exercises lovingkindness, justice, and righteousness on earth; for I delight in these things," declares the Lord.*"

Could it be stated, "let not a sovereign God boast of His sovereignty?

Any boasting should only be regarding the understanding and knowledge of God Himself. The word "understands" comes from a root word that means "prudent." It can include the concept of "experience." In the New Testament, Matthew 25: 1-13 is the parable of the Ten Virgins, five foolish and five prudent. The word in Greek for "prudent" means "to consider the thoughts of another, to catch the mind of." The word for "knows" is the Hebrew "yada" (transliterated). It means "to know." In the New Testament, the Greek "ginosko" means "to come to know, or to ascertain knowledge and understanding by experience." In both Old and New Testaments God wants us to understand and know Him. This involves much more than having a collection of facts about God, but to have experienced Him and through that experience find the intimacy of a relationship. Satanic, worldly kings never seem to want others to know them intimately for fear someone will discover weakness and use it against them. God has no weaknesses and

How Does God Express His Sovereignty?

desires His children to have that intimacy with Him. We are to come to Him as a child.

Lovingkindness, justice, righteousness...the things which delight Him. These are the characteristics displayed of the Sovereign God on earth. Please note that there is no concept of control in any of those words. The meaning of "exercises" is simply "do, make." These things are what God does. Another aspect of righteousness means "blameless conduct, and integrity" God never sins and can always be trusted. The meaning of "justice" is:

(CWSB Dictionary) "*H4941.* מִשְׁפָּט *mišpāṭ: A masculine noun meaning a judgment, a legal decision, a legal case, a claim, proper, rectitude. The word connotes several variations in meanings depending on the context. It is used to describe a legal decision or judgment rendered: it describes a legal decision given by God to be followed by the people (Isa. 58:2; Zeph. 2:3; Mal. 2:17). These decisions could come through the use of the Urim and Thummim (Num. 27:21). The high priest wore a pouch called the breastpiece of justice, containing the Urim and Thummim by which decisions were obtained from the Lord (Ex. 28:30). Doing what was right and just in the Lord's eyes was far more important than presenting sacrifices to Him (Gen. 18:19; Prov. 21:3, 15). God was declared to be the Judge of the whole earth who rendered justice faithfully (Gen. 18:25; Isa. 30:18). In the plural form, the word describes legal judgments, cases, examples, laws, and specifications.*"

Lovingkindness is a combination of love and kindness (remember from above that the meaning of "grace" is "kindness").

Ezekiel 33:11a (NASB) "*[11] Say to them, 'As I live!' declares the Lord God, 'I take no pleasure in the death of*

How Does God Express His Sovereignty?

the wicked, but rather that the wicked turn from his way and live..."

Here in Ezekiel, we see that God has no pleasure in anyone's death even though some religious philosophies twist this into God declaring before Adam existed who is going to spend eternity in the torment of the lake of fire. Thank you, but, I'll stick with what God really says and not Satan's twist on things. Another interesting item in this verse is the phrase "Lord God." The word for "Lord" comes from a root word meaning "sovereign." The actual word is transliterated as "Adonay," and is usually translated "Lord." This is part of the reason I believe there is a "sovereign" aspect of God – I just don't believe in the satanic and fleshly embellishment that usually goes along with it. In the Hebrew, "sovereign" simply means "kingdom", and by implication, "ruler." The existence of the word does not require any exaggeration. But, back to the point, God's attitude about death – that is something that comes from within Him and pervades everything about Him. That is why He sent His Son to die for the sins of the whole world. And we are to imitate Him. This is simply one of His ways.

Ezekiel 22:30-31 contains a description of one of God's ways that is embedded in our praying, that hardly anyone pays any attention.

Ezekiel 22:30-31 (NASB)" *[30] I searched for a man among them who would build up the wall and stand in the gap before Me for the land, so that I would not destroy it; but I found no one. [31] Thus I have poured out My indignation on them; I have consumed them with the fire of My wrath; their way I have brought upon their heads," declares the Lord God."*

God's way includes our participation in what God is doing (build up the wall, stand in the gap). If you carefully

How Does God Express His Sovereignty?

study the word "abide" in 1 John 2, you will find about a dozen times where God does the abiding, about as many times where the saint does the abiding, and again, almost the same number of times where the abiding takes place on the part of both God and the saint. This concept of participation, or standing in the gap, is also illustrated in the following:

Exodus 32:9-10 (NASB) *"9 The Lord said to Moses, "I have seen this people, and behold, they are an obstinate people. 10 Now then let Me alone, that My anger may burn against them and that I may destroy them; and I will make of you a great nation.""*

In the next few verses, Moses talks with God and identifies some points that are important. God destroying the Israelites would give Gentiles cause to "bad-mouth" God, and it might go against the unconditional covenant God made with Abraham, Isaac, and Jacob. Then in verse 14, God relented, changed his mind, and did not destroy them. (Note God still got the end result, but it took 40 years for the rebellious ones to die off in the wilderness.) Here we see that Moses was "standing in the gap" on behalf of the Israelites. If no one was there to stand in the gap, they would have been destroyed as indicated in Ezekiel 22:31.

It is very important to God that we are willing and active participants in what is his will, the things which make him happy, the things which please him. This is another one of God's ways, participation with others, not individual isolation.

How Does God Express His Sovereignty?

God Is A Warrior

In the BHS Hebrew text, the phrase "Lord of hosts" is used about 256 times, and "God of hosts" is used about 15 times. I find in many various writings that since God is the "Lord of hosts" that He is the one in total overall control of everything. Unfortunately, the idea of being in control because of assumptions in a name is not very reliable or trustworthy – "control" is being read into the Scripture. There is only one of the 256 verses that give us a clue about "how" God expresses His "Lord of hosts" name. That verse is Isaiah 42:13:

Isaiah 42:13 (NASB) "*13 The Lord will go forth like a warrior, He will arouse His zeal like a man of war. He will utter a shout, yes, He will raise a war cry. He will prevail against His enemies.*"

This verse identifies that God uses His voice to express His being "Lord of hosts." The word "warrior" (think exaggeration and embellishment) at the beginning of this verse simply means "strong and mighty." The Lord will go forth strong and mighty. An illustration of this is in Revelation

Revelation 19:15 (NASB) "*15 From His mouth comes a sharp sword, so that with it He may strike down the nations, and He will rule them with a rod of iron; and He treads the wine press of the fierce wrath of God, the Almighty.*"

The way God behaves as a warrior is simply to use His voice. This passage in Revelation corresponds perfectly to one item in the full armor of God in Ephesians chapter 6, "the sword of the Spirit, which is the word of God." Proverbs 18:21 tells us the tongue has the power of life

How Does God Express His Sovereignty?

and death. It is too easy to take our current modern English concepts and superimpose them onto the Scriptures. It is too easy to assume that because God is named "Lord of hosts," that God is a control freak without paying attention to His ways, and what is actually stated in Scripture. Being a control freak is a way of the flesh and Satan and is definitely not godly.

God wins wars by speaking, raising a war cry, not acting in control the way our current society thinks of control. Genesis chapter 1 is a fantastic example of what God can do simply by speaking. Scripture does not show God ever lifts a shovel to create a mountain, or sets foot on earth and wields a physical sword to hack people to death by swinging his arm. God's way is to speak, not control or physically manipulate people. The only references where God would use his hands was to form the animals and Adam and Eve. The word "formed" in Genesis 1 and 2 is the same word used for a potter that "forms" pottery on a wheel with his hands. That word is not used about God for things that are not animals or people, and it is only related to creation.

How Does God Express His Sovereignty?

Control Can Be Satanic

Matthew 20:25-28 (NASB) "*25 But Jesus called them to Himself and said, "You know that the rulers of the Gentiles lord it over them, and their great men exercise authority over them. 26 It is not this way among you, but whoever wishes to become great among you shall be your servant, 27 and whoever wishes to be first among you shall be your slave; 28 just as the Son of Man did not come to be served, but to serve, and to give His life a ransom for many."* " (See also Luke 22:25-26)

Many people will read this passage and only focus on the idea that the greatest in the kingdom is the servant of all. They suppress the beginning of this passage and exaggerate only the one point. Jesus is presenting a contrast here between Satan's kingdom, represented by the kings or rulers of the Gentiles, and the ways of the kingdom of God. The worldly kings "lord it over" their people, which means that they "exercise authority over" their people, i.e. those kings control and oppress their people. Oppression is from the devil as stated in Acts 10:38 ("oppress"* means "to exercise power over another"). The contrast comes next with the words: "It is not this way among you" (i.e. the disciples). This obviously shows that God's kingdom behaves very differently than the "control freaks" of the satanic world system. I use the term "satanic" because the kingdoms of the world had been given to Satan as described in the temptations given by Satan to Jesus (Matthew 4:1-11). This shows another way that God expresses His Sovereignty. NOT by oppression, exercising power over people, but by being the greatest servant of all. That in itself is an extreme opposite of what many people identify as "sovereignty." Jesus came to be a servant, not to be served as the satanic

How Does God Express His Sovereignty?

world kingdoms operate. One of the more disturbing things I've read in the Sovereignty writings is that too much of the descriptions are a closer match to human despotic leaders like Attila the Hun, Genghis Kahn, Hitler, Stalin, Lenin, Pol Pot, Idi Amin, than to a loving God who sent His Son to die for our sins.

There are several other characteristics of God mentioned in several places throughout the Scriptures. Genesis 24:27, 32:10 identifies kindness and faithfulness. Holy is identified in Leviticus 11:44-45 and 1 Peter 1:16 – we are to be holy because He is holy (meaning "set apart, sanctified, consecrated, and is the root for the word "saint"). Matthew 5:48 identifies God is perfect (not lacking any moral quality, complete, full, not wanting in anything) and we are to be perfect also. Malachi 3:6 and Hebrews 3:8 tell us He does not change, He is the same yesterday, today, and forever. There is a remarkable consistency to Him. 2 Chronicles 19:7 and Romans 2:11 tell us that God does not show partiality or favoritism, and James 2:9 tells us that we are not to show partiality either.

God's way is NOT to control people - that is Satan's way. God can control other things as detailed in my book, "Six Biblical Issues Against "God Is In Control"." Please refer to that book for an extensive examination of the concept of control. Theologians who think that God controls people do not dictate to God how He is to act and behave. God reveals how and why He acts and behaves the way He does through teaching us His ways.

*A further note on the word "oppress." The word "control" means "to cause someone or something to behave a certain way or believe a certain thing." The word "cause" means "a person or thing that gives rise to an action, phenomenon, or condition." This obviously shows that

How Does God Express His Sovereignty?

"oppress" (exercise power over another) and "control" are equivalent concepts, directly interchangeable. When you hear someone say the phrase "God is in control," particularly in reference to people (even themselves), you should now recognize that as a blasphemous statement - taking something that is obviously satanic and applying it to God. That is not God's way... God's way is the way of the Servant. In homes and other places where there are servants, isn't it the case that the servants are the ones that get things done?

How Does God Express His Sovereignty?

Sovereignty Twists

I have rarely found anything mentioned in the Sovereignty writings regarding any other characteristics of God other than "control," and "sovereignty." Rarely is love ever mentioned in those writings. John Calvin mentions several places that it is out of God's kindness that He assigns some to eternity in the lake of fire... **Kindness**?!?!

One of the most ignored aspects of Romans chapter 9 is the context (actually chapters 9 to 11). Paul begins chapter 9 with the wish that his fellow Israelites would come to know Jesus as Messiah (paraphrasing). Paul then goes on to describe with parables or metaphors how God has dealt with those Israelites historically and points out through these three chapters that God has not abandoned the Israelites. Please note that the Israelites were already Israelites for over 400 years before God began dealing with them in the manner pictured by Paul. They became Israelites when God changed Jacob's name to Israel. Many of the verses in Romans 9 are twisted out of context to mean how people become regenerate, or born again, by God making the decision way ahead of time. The contextual fact that the Israelites were Israelites for over 400 years BEFORE God began dealing with them means that what is being pictured is not how people became part of the group called "Israelites," but how He handled those who are ALREADY Israelites. This takes the idea completely out of contention that these verses could be used to support God determining ahead of time who would be in heaven or hell. God always chooses those who are already part of an existing membership, not who is going to comprise the membership. That membership comes from personal choice, not God forcing or coercing people into that membership. We will see this

How Does God Express His Sovereignty?

illustrated in the following verse discussions beginning with the misunderstanding of Romans 9:15:

Romans 9:15 (NASB) "*¹⁵ For He says to Moses, "I will have mercy on whom I have mercy, and I will have compassion on whom I have compassion."* "

The Sovereignty writings use this to indicate the absolute control God has over people's eternal destiny. There is a real problem with using this verse for that conclusion, aside from it being out of context with Paul's stated intent. There is a word in Greek that is used about 175 times in 160 verses, but, it is never translated. The basic issue is that there are no words in English that can be used in a word-for-word translation - it would require a phrase of about 7-9 words to get the meaning across. Translators only want to use one or two words in translation, and rarely three, more than that is an indicator of a poor translator. Including the meaning of that word makes that verse read: "...I will have mercy, conditional on circumstances, on those who might have mercy, and I will have compassion, conditional on circumstances, on those who might have compassion." Here is the lexicon definition of that missing word:

Romans 9:15 (NA28) "*¹⁵ τῷ Μωϋσεῖ γὰρ λέγει· ἐλεήσω ὃν ἂν ἐλεῶ καὶ οἰκτιρήσω ὃν ἂν οἰκτίρω.*"

(CWSB Dictionary) "*302. ἄv án; particle used with the opt., subjunctive, and indic. moods; sometimes properly rendered by "perhaps"; more commonly not expressed in Eng. by any corresponding particle, but only giving to a proposition or sentence a <u>stamp of uncertainty and mere possibility, and indicating a dependence on circumstances.</u> In this way it serves to <u>modify or strengthen the intrinsic force of the opt. and subjunctive</u> while it can also, similarly, affect the meaning of the indic. (the pres. and perf. excepted) and other verbal forms. This particle stands after one or more words in a clause and is thus distinguished from án*

How Does God Express His Sovereignty?

for eán (G1437), if." Additionally, the second use of "mercy" and "compassion" in that verse is in the subjunctive mood which introduces an element of doubt to the word - ergo the use of "might have" in my rendering. Note in the definition of ἄν, " it serves to modify or strengthen the intrinsic force of the opt., and subjunctive ." This verse is NOT an absolute statement, but a statement indicating that the mercy and compassion of God is extremely dependent on the circumstances which completely removes it from any support of God making eternal destiny decisions way back when before any of us were born based on His Sovereignty and control. God's "Sovereignty"" and "control" does not control our eternal destiny.

Another Sovereignty issue that has its own built-in twists is in Romans 9:18, 21-23. Verse 18 is interpreted from the basis of control with no respect to God's use of persuasion (the root word for faith and believe) and the context of the Israelites being Israelites for over 400 years before God started dealing with them this way. Control is being "read into" verse 18, completely ignoring God's ways.

The "potter" dialog is another aspect with its own built-in twists. The apparently volatile aspect of this is the concept of vessels for "honor" versus vessels for "dishonor." There are three passages where Paul talks about "honor" versus "dishonor." These are 1 Cor. 12:11-27, 2 Tim. 2:20-23, in addition to this passage in Romans. Rarely are the other two passages referenced in the Sovereignty writings. I'm one to pay attention to all the contexts, not just a few words in isolation.

Romans 9:21 (NASB) "*²¹ Or does not the potter have a right over the clay, to make from the same lump one*

How Does God Express His Sovereignty?

vessel for honorable use and another for common use?"

2 Timothy 2:20-21 (NASB) *"[20] Now in a large house there are not only gold and silver vessels, but also vessels of wood and of earthenware, and some to honor and some to dishonor. [21] Therefore, if anyone cleanses himself from these things, he will be a vessel for honor, sanctified, useful to the Master, prepared for every good work."*

1 Corinthians 12:22-25 (NASB) *"[22] On the contrary, it is much truer that the members of the body which seem to be weaker are necessary; [23] and those members of the body which we deem less honorable, on these we bestow more abundant honor, and our less presentable members become much more presentable, [24] whereas our more presentable members have no need of it. But God has so composed the body, giving more abundant honor to that member which lacked, [25] so that there may be no division in the body, but that the members may have the same care for one another."*

The Timothy passage identifies that both types of vessels are already in the same house, God's house. Of the few Sovereignty writers that mention this passage, they identify that within the same house are both saved and unsaved. I wonder how they fit that with Jesus statement that a house divided against itself cannot stand. And if the house of God is filled with both saved and unsaved, how would anyone determine the difference?

The Corinthian passage identifies that members of the body of Christ can be vessels of dishonor (the basic requirement for membership in the body is being saved already). Somehow all three passages have to fit together; otherwise, there is a very serious contradiction within Scripture.

The resolution is very easy and simple. God molds

How Does God Express His Sovereignty?

both vessels from the same "lump" of clay. If you research the word in the Greek for "lump," it becomes self-evident that the lump has already been mixed and is now ready for use. When clay is dug up from the ground, it must first be broken up into as fine a powder as possible, fully mixed with water and set aside to "rest" for up to a couple months for the moisture content to become consistent throughout before it can be used for pottery. If the moisture is not consistent throughout, then when it is fired, the clay will dry out at different rates in various spots and cause the vessel to crack, becoming unfit for any use. That simply means that God is using people who have already been born again for making these different vessels. (The word in Greek for "vessels" is most frequently used as a metaphor for "people" in both Scripture and secular writings.)

    Here again, we see that the truth of Scripture indicates that God makes His choices from members of an existing group, not to mention the overriding context of the Israelites already being Israelites over 400 years for Paul's illustrations. None of His choices are from a nondescript population to become members of a group. The Sovereignty writings assume because God must be in control, that the choices are for the group membership, not for what role the members are to play. Since God does not control any person's eternal destiny, then God does not define, nor predefine, the members of the group. The real point of "predestination" is what God desires of those who will become members of His family once they are members, not who becomes members of the family. God has demonstrated His love for us and is waiting for us to choose to demonstrate our love for Him.

    This is also demonstrated in Luke 6:12-13 where Jesus prayed all night and in the morning called all the

How Does God Express His Sovereignty?

disciples together, and from that existing group membership, chose the twelve apostles. The Twelve were not just random selections from the general population walking the streets of Israelite towns and villages but from an established group membership.

How Does God Express His Sovereignty?

Context Is Everything, And Then Some...

I would be greatly surprised to find someone in the United States, an adult, who has never heard the phrase "context is everything." That phrase has been around for such a long time and has been misused and abused so much, that no one really pays attention to it anymore. Even though that phrase may seem trite and worn, it is just as true now as it was when it was first spoken.

The church today does not teach anything related to what the context is for the Christian living today, nor did it a couple centuries ago. There are two major contexts that we need to pay attention to, and I'm not talking about the Old Testament and the New Testament. I'm talking about simple "good" and "evil," that is found in both Testaments. Sin entered humanity in that context. Born again believers are not currently taught about what their context is and how to operate and function within their context. Jesus, in what many label "The Great Commission," identified two things that need to be done; baptize the new believer, and teach them to observe all that Jesus had commanded. My book, "Discipling A New Believer, by Larry Adams" identifies over 70 items that Jesus made a command regarding. That is just the beginning.

God's word is life (John 6:63). And,

James 1:22 (NASB) "[22] *But prove yourselves doers of the word, and not merely hearers who delude themselves.*"

Fellowship and Bible study are extremely important to how we are to behave in the context of good versus

How Does God Express His Sovereignty?

evil. In order to be a Christian we do not have to become a member of a local congregation – that is not part of believing on Jesus by faith. However,

Hebrews 10:25 (NASB) "[25] *not forsaking our own assembling together, as is the habit of some, but encouraging one another; and all the more as you see the day drawing near.*"

Fellowship is important if for no other reason that we are to find encouragement from other believers. Several allegories are used in the New Testament to describe the Christian life. Paul uses "running a race," "fighting the good fight," to describe the life he has led in following Christ. Jesus told us that in this life here on Earth we would have trials and tribulations – not a "la-la-land rose petals everywhere" kind of life (John 16:33). Encouragement from other believers helps keep us focused on what God's purpose is in our life.

The Bible is where we find God's principles and concepts by which we are to live our life. There are approximately 31,100 verses in the Bible. No one is going to get all the possible understanding of all those verses overnight, possibly not in their entire lifetime. The point is not to get the total understanding possible as quickly as possible, but to be persistent in studying the Bible so that we can continually strengthen our relationship with God. In the Greek, the word for "know" (and it's various forms) is "ginosko" (transliterated). The basic meaning of ginosko is "to come to know." Think about that meaning for a minute – it is NOT just having knowledge of whatever sort. "To come to" means that you are NOT at a certain place or position and by some process, you come to another place or position. Ginosko means that "we ascertain knowledge and understanding by means of experience." We need to

How Does God Express His Sovereignty?

study the Bible, have fellowship with other believers, and spend dedicated time in prayer. All these are the means of experience that bring us to the place and position of "knowing" God, and being "known" by God – it works both ways. Both God and ourselves need to have experience with each other. In 1 John 2, if you study the word "abide" (meaning to dwell or live in/at), there are about a dozen places that identify God doing the abiding, about as many where the saint is doing the abiding, and almost as many times the abiding is a joint effort of both the saint and God. God wants us to participate in our Christian life, a lot more than just praying a prayer of salvation, or saying "grace" over dinner.

Another part of our Christian life context presents itself in just about every situation we find ourselves in. The situation does not need to be a major catastrophe, many times it only seems insignificant. Hebrews 5:14 tells us that we are to have our senses trained to discern good and evil, and it takes practice. Over and over again we are confronted with decisions. Many times those decisions do not seem very different from a moral perspective, and they may not be very different. Other times it looks like the proverbial "lesser of two evils." These decisions are the "practice" we go through to have our senses trained to discern good and evil.

One prevalent attitude I find is that Christians think that the situations we go through rarely seem morally or spiritually significant. It comes across as God only attempts to teach them about Bible things or moral things once in a long while. It's as though the Holy Spirit comes and visits a couple times a month, instead of living within us. These "practice" situations could realistically happen several times a day. The Holy Spirit, our Comforter, Teach-

How Does God Express His Sovereignty?

er, Guide (John 14 & 16), is with us constantly and never leaves us.

As unbelievers, we were all alone with ourselves, having to make our own moral and life decisions. When we are born-again, we need the Holy Spirit with us constantly because we have never before been in this kind of spiritual environment. We have no way of knowing ahead of time what it is like or how to navigate within our new heavenly environment here on Earth. Superficially, things may look the same, but morally and spiritually things are completely different. The Bible is our "handbook" so to speak, and as a new believer, we know nothing about it or how it applies to life. We need the Holy Spirit with us constantly to navigate this strange new life. One of the deeds of the flesh we need to put to death is the habit of always making our own decisions based on our former worldly ways of doing things (Romans 8:13; Colossians 3:5).

In John 11:38-44 we have the situation of Lazarus being raised from the grave. The interesting point is that Lazarus stumbled out of the grave wrapped in grave clothes and Jesus stated: "Unbind him." This is a good illustration of what it is like when we are born again. While an unbeliever, we are dead (separated from God) in our sins, and in bondage (bound) to our sins. When we are born again, we, like Lazarus, are wrapped in grave clothes, all wrapped up in the world's way of doing things and ways of thinking. We need to be "unbound" from the ways of the world. We need to be taught the ways of the kingdom of God. That teaching is our being "unbound" from our former worldly ways. Learning our "context" should be part of the process of being "unbound."

Prayer is another part of the context of a Christian. Jesus frequently prayed, going off to a solitary place,

How Does God Express His Sovereignty?

sometimes for the entire night. See Mark 1:35; Matthew 11:25-26, 14:33; Luke 6:12, 21: 41-44, 22:34. Paul tells us to pray without ceasing in 1 Thessalonians 5:17. That does not mean the only thing we do is pray. It means that when there is a need that we bring before God, it becomes something that we remember each time we pray until we have the answer. We might pray once or twice a day and each time that is one of the items in each prayer time. Prayer is more than saying "grace" at meals, it is humbling ourselves before God regarding how great God is and how much He loves us, and how much we need to depend on His still small voice to lead us and guide us through everything we have to deal with in this life on Earth. Our life as an unbeliever was signified by being our own god, making all the decisions and attempting in the strength of our flesh and the ingenuity of our minds to determine goals and achieve them. As believers, we now have given our lives to Christ (God), and we are to live for him. A popular verse that is frequently misquoted and misapplied is the one about "all things work together for good..."

Romans 8:28 (NASB) "[28] *And we know that God causes all things to work together for good to those who love God, to those who are called according to His purpose.*"

Notice that there is a phrase at the end of that verse, and if you listen carefully to people who quote this often, that last phrase is frequently left out. Actually, there are two phrases at the end that need careful attention. "...to those who love God, to those who are called according to His purpose." These two phases are really two requirements for things to work together for good. Those requirements are 1) love God; 2) be called according to HIS purpose. That also means that things may not work together for good if we desire our own satisfaction above God's purpose for our lives. The real problem with that verse is found in the Greek text. It

How Does God Express His Sovereignty?

states: " But know the love of God for the truly called/invited, works with everything, toward the good, in accordance with his plan/purpose." In the Greek text, there is no indication of any requirements to be performed by the believer in order to get God to work all things for good. God works to accomplish His purpose based on His love only. This is a typically badly translated verse. God's love does not come with requirements. While we were sinners and not capable of doing anything to earn His love, He loved us and sent His son to die for us; no requirements on our part were required.

James 4:3 (NASB) "*³ You ask and do not receive, because you ask with wrong motives, so that you may spend it on your pleasures.*"

John 9:31 (NASB) "*³¹ We know that God does not hear sinners; but if anyone is God-fearing and does His will, He hears him.*"

When we become born-again believers, our lives are not our own anymore – Jesus paid the penalty for our sin on the cross, and that is the purchase price for our lives – 1 Corinthians 6:20. We are no longer slaves to sin, but that requires that instead of being our own god, we now have to be slaves to God, we have been bought with a price. The twist in this is that by being a slave to God, we also find freedom, not only from the burden and bondage to sin but also the freedom to be what God originally intended mankind to be. Finding salvation in Christ is literally being dragged out of hell and into God's kingdom of light, love, and eternal life. We find that what is best for ourselves is to deny ourselves and embrace God's ways. Prayer is one of the strongest means of making that transition. Along with prayer, as already mentioned, are things like fellowship and Bible study.

In Ephesians 6, Paul identifies the full armor of God, ending with praying in the Spirit. Praying in the Spirit is how

How Does God Express His Sovereignty?

we get to the Throne. Satan's schemes will be designed to interfere with or prohibit your use of what God has given you. We fight through praying in the Spirit. That means we stand before God on His throne on the basis of the Gospel of Peace (shoes, peace with God that was made by the sacrifice of Jesus on the cross and His resurrection). We have a heart intent to pursue righteousness (breastplate), based on the truth of God's Word (belt). Our minds are transformed by the work of the Holy Spirit (helmet), and we have a firm resolution and persuasion in our hearts and minds that God is for us. And, that faith will overcome everything the enemy throws at us (shield of faith). We know God's word, the Bible (the sword of the Spirit), and are able to listen to the still small voice of the Lord for what of the Bible applies to any specific situation (scheme, attack of the enemy). We are able to speak that truth into the situation by prayer in the Spirit – all these items are used in prayer in the Spirit. We know that the war is in the "second heaven", and we are before the throne in the "third heaven", simply requesting that the victory in Christ be applied to the situation at hand.

Prayer really "works." Many things can interfere with prayer like harboring sin in our lives, or placing our own fleshly desires ahead of God's purpose in our life. Or attempting to accomplish God's will in our life by our own fleshly strength and the ingenuity of our own minds instead of following the Spirit and letting the power of the Spirit accomplish God's goals in God's way. Primarily, prayer changes us – God already knows what is needed and when. Prayer keeps us in contact and communication with God so that we can participate with Him in the way He wants things to take place.

Knowing God's commands, God's will, God's ways, God's voice, God's word, Bible study, fellowship, and prayer are the means by which we learn how God wants us to function and behave in the context of good and evil we find ourselves in. God teaches us these things in such a way that it is not overwhelming, but as we can handle things and changes are made in our lives, He gives us a little bit more. It is a process of experience, not a sudden download of a new app and its appropriate data files. It is a transformation, not an eradication and replacement. If you want your marriage to be successful, you must invest time and effort into it. Our relationship with God requires the same. We have a mortal enemy, Satan. There are temptations and strong persuasions to choose the path of evil instead of good or righteousness. Paul in Ephesians 6 tells us that the full armor of God is so we can stand in the face of Satan's schemes against us. How well do you think you could stand if you are only partially clothed in His armor and have no strength of relationship to Him?

How Does God Express His Sovereignty?

In Summary...

The primary focus of this discussion has been to identify what God says about Himself, His personality, character, how He does what He does and why He does it the way it gets done. People's ideas and opinions do not matter because we are told in Scripture that His ways are higher (more excellent) that our ways, and we cannot figure them out - God must teach them to us.

In this discussion, we have identified many characteristics of God that help us identify His ways, and we are commanded to know His ways. His ways are just, and the righteous are to walk in them. God's ways are a fantastic insight into who God is, His personality and character, that we have no other means of finding out. God will teach the humble His ways (since we cannot figure them out by our own fleshly strength or the ingenuity of our own minds). He is the comforter, the one called alongside to help, teach and guide. He is humble and meek, thirsty for righteousness, and merciful. He does not have an arrogant spiritual attitude. He is a peacemaker, and endures persecution. He exercises lovingkindness without preconditions or requirements. He shows justice and righteousness on Earth. He is not boastful. He desires knowledge and understanding of himself founded on intimate experience. God desires that we turn from our own ways instead of choosing the path of death. He does not "Lord it over" his own, the opposite of the satanic world system way of the kings and rulers of the Earth.

God is kind, faithful, holy, perfect (not lacking in any moral quality), unchanging, and does not show partiality. And underlying all of these characteristics and ways, He is love, and desires for us to be the same.

The question should arise by this time, "If all these

How Does God Express His Sovereignty?

ways have been identified, is there anything left for God to teach me?" Remember that I stated that just knowing a bunch of facts doesn't cut it? The most difficult part is yet to come. The real teaching part is applying any or all of these to specific situations. That's where the ability to listen to the still small voice of the Lord comes into play. Knowing facts is very different from the wisdom of how to apply those facts in any specific situation.

Listening to God's voice is important in both Testaments, almost required. When we listen, there are blessings, when we don't, we are cursed. Yes, there is a verse that talks about a curse without a cause will not alight, but not listening happens to be a cause that brings a curse. Jesus identified in John 10:27 that his sheep hear his voice... Did you get that? Hear His voice? That is one of the things I identified that is largely ignored in the church today, to our own detriment. Listing all these characteristics and ways of God is only the first step, and there may be more ways revealed by Him. Use this listing as a beginning reference, and be careful not to suppress characteristics or attributes of these in their context. That's as bad as not listening to His voice.

In general, we could summarize God's ways as the ways of a servant, not anything like a human despotic dictator. Theologians of the Dark Ages took the limitations and fleshly characteristics of how people function and why they do things the way they do and applied those characteristics to God. We are created in God's image and likeness, but we are a limited creation and our limitations do not limit God. Our limitations and being finite (God is infinite) are the simple reason that we cannot figure out God's ways and God must teach us His ways.

God has an amazing propensity for patience, and we can be thankful for that over the years He will be teaching us.

How Does God Express His Sovereignty?

(Get that? YEARS!) At his writing, I'm only a few weeks short of walking with the Lord for 57 years. I'm still learning. Every situation turns out to be a new adventure in experiencing God. Another of His characteristics is that He never "grows old." God gave me the gift of teaching, and if life on earth is the "training ground" for eternity, then I'll be a teacher for eternity and never run out of something to teach about God. I have to seriously consider that my time on earth (in training) is nowhere near enough even to get close to knowing all God's ways, and to get to know Him for who He really is. This journey is called "eternal life," and it takes an eternity to get through it.

God wants us to be conformed to the image of his son (Romans 8:29). God wants us to be participants with him on this eternal journey. Being taught his ways is how we find out what is the image of his son that he wants us to be. His ways, personality, and character show us how he expresses his sovereignty. That's how I want to be when I grow up...

www.ingramcontent.com/pod-product-compliance
Lightning Source LLC
Chambersburg PA
CBHW031505040426
42444CB00007B/1218